POWER HOUSE

SCIENCE ACTIVITIES FOR CHILDREN

ALISON ALEXANDER and SUSIE BOWER

Illustrated by Carolyn Scrace

COLLINS

POWER HOUSE

The aim of this book is to encourage children to explore ways of harnessing and using energy.

By making insects creep, and dancers dance, or through building a paper house, children can discover how forces and energy are used in machines.

Specially chosen to appeal to 6 – 10 year olds, the experiments are simple and safe. Using equipment mostly found around the home, they utilize the manipulative skills and abilities of this age group.

This book with its lively illustrations and easy-to-follow instructions will stimulate young children to adapt and develop their own variations of the experiments – an important point in the education of today's child.

Important note
Masking tape

We have recommended using what is known in this country as masking tape as opposed to Sellotape. This is because it is easy to tear and stick, it can be painted over and it is fairly water resistant.

William Collins Sons & Co Ltd
London · Glasgow · Sydney · Auckland
Toronto · Johannesburg

First published 1991

A CIP catalogue record for this book is available from the British Library
ISBN 0 00 184845 3 (hardback)
ISBN 0 00 196400 3 (paperback)

Printed and bound in Hong Kong
Set in 12/14 Gill sans

Contents

Make a Boat that Goes like a Rocket

You will need:

- small plastic or polystyrene tray such as those used for packing food in supermarkets
- 2 flexible drinking straws
- 2 balloons
- masking tape
- Blu-Tak/Plasticine/bulldog clip
- sheet of paper
- pencil
- jam jar lid
- scissors

Make two small holes in one end of the tray large enough for the straws to fit through.

Fix the balloons on the end of the straws nearest the bendy part and seal with tape. Test that the join is airtight by blowing up the balloons through the straws. This will also soften the balloons and make them easier to blow up later.

Next slide the straws through the holes so that the balloons are resting in the tray.

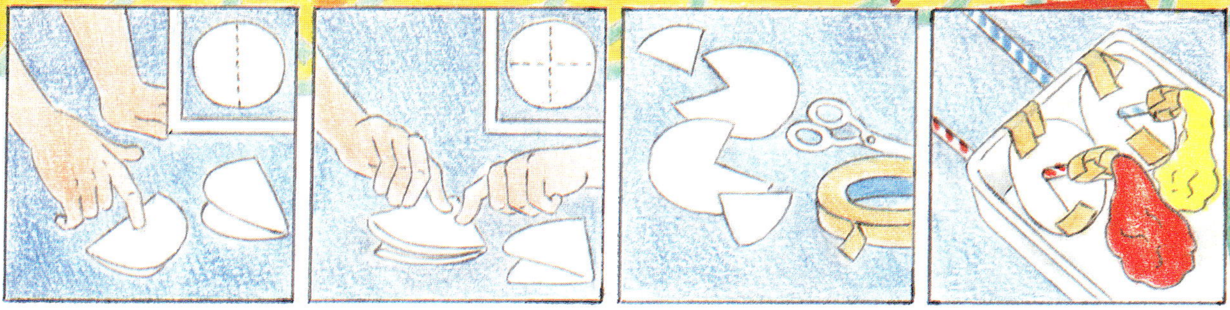

To make funnels to hold the balloons steady in the boat, use the jam jar lid as a template and draw two circles on the sheet of paper. Cut them out as shown and tape them round the straws to form funnels. Then tape them to the side of the tray to keep them in place.

Blow up one balloon and seal the end of the straw with Blu-Tak. Then blow up the other balloon and seal that. Lower the boat into the water and remove the Blu-Tak so that the boat can set off.

Why it works
As the air stored in the balloons rushes out through the straws, the boat is pushed forward in the opposite direction. In the same way jet engines and rockets are propelled forward by the escaping gases from the burning fuel.

Fly a Kite that Never Fails

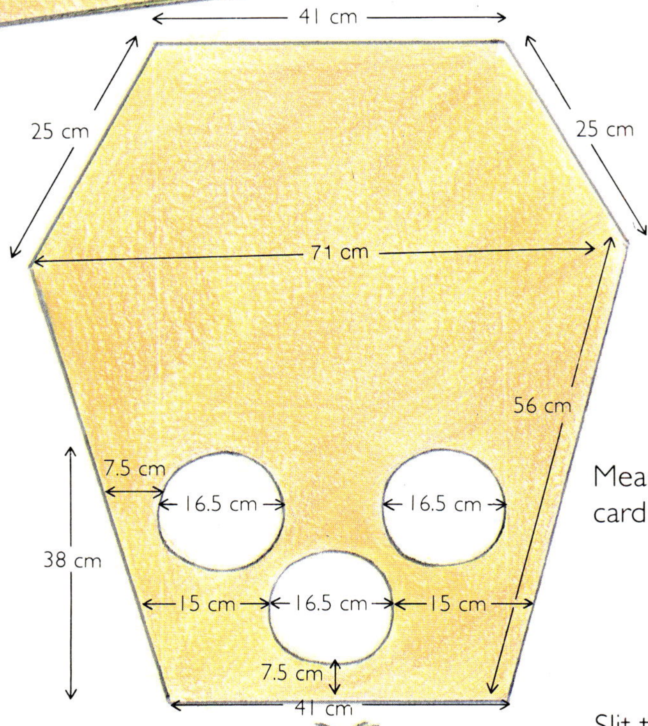

You will need:

strong dustbin liner
2 plant support sticks or similar
  approx 76 cm long
scissors
ball of string
large sheet of card or stiff paper
  approx 76 x 76 cm
insulating tape
tape measure

Measure and draw the kite pattern on the card following the diagram, then cut it out.

Slit the dustbin liner down one side and across the bottom and open it out flat. Lay the pattern on top of the liner, taping it down all round to keep it in place. Then cut out the kite. Do not forget the holes.

Using insulating tape, fix the sticks in position, then make two small holes for the string by pinching up the liner and snipping it across. They will need to be strengthened and to do this, fold pieces of tape around the edges as shown. Tie a piece of string about 90 cm long between the two small holes then tie a knot in the middle to form a loop about 8 –10 cm long. Now tie the loose end of your ball of string to the loop.

You can decorate the kite using paints or pieces of self-adhesive coloured paper.

To fly the kite, face into the wind and hold the kite behind you (or get a friend to help). Start running, letting go of the kite and letting the string out as the wind catches it. If it is not very windy the kite will stay up as long as you keep the string short and keep running.

Why it works

Although you cannot feel it, the air all around us pushes against anything it touches. The design of a kite affects the way the air moves and pushes around it. This kite is designed to fly at an angle so that there is more air flowing below it than above. This means there is a greater force pushing upwards than downwards, so the kite stays up.

Waterworks

You will need:
empty washing-up liquid carton
plastic straw
scissors
masking tape
pencil
corkscrew

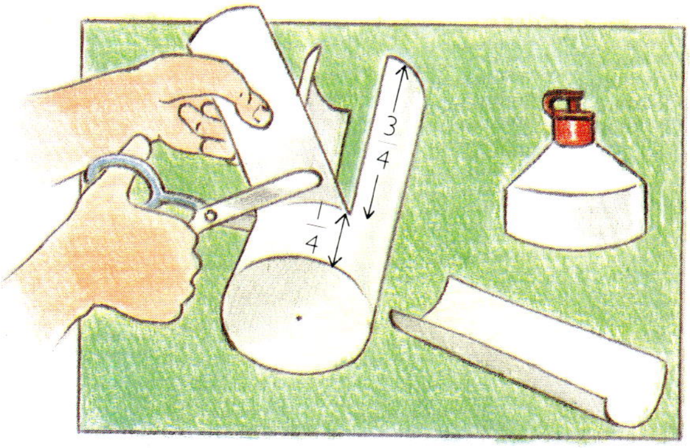

Cut the top off the carton and then cut two panels out of each side as shown.

To make the funnel, remove the lid from the top of the carton. Then turn the top upside down and tape it securely to the sides of the carton so that it is at an angle.

Using the corkscrew, make two holes opposite each other in the side panels of the carton. Smooth the ragged edges by pushing the pencil through the hole and twisting it around. This is so that the straw will turn freely when pushed through.

To make the wheel, use the panels from the carton. Cut four pieces approximately 6 cm x 4 cm, fold them in half lengthwise and tape them together to form a wheel as shown. The size of the wheel will depend on the size of the carton. It must be able to spin freely.

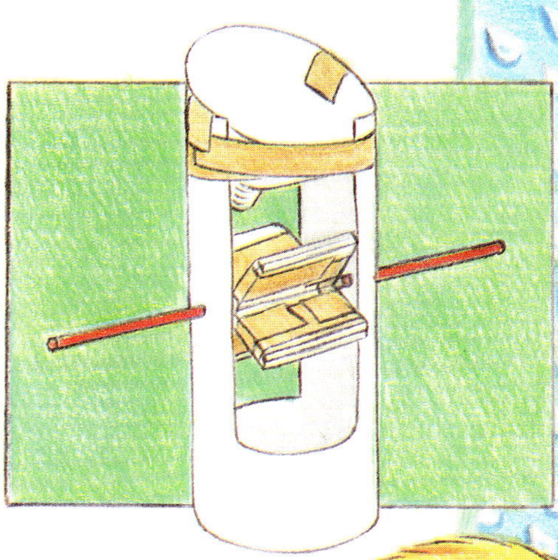

Push one end of the straw through one of the holes in the side of the carton, then through the centre of the wheel and through the hole on the other side. Tape the wheel so that it is firmly fixed to the straw and moves with it.

Pour water down the funnel and the wheel will turn. You could try putting string round a small yogurt pot and attaching it to the straw to see if the wheel will wind it up.

Why it works
The force of the falling water makes the wheel turn. This energy can then be harnessed to power any machinery or object attached to the wheel axle.

Take All Your Things Upstairs .

You will need:
2 cotton reels
2 plant support sticks
ball of string
carrier bag
masking tape
Blu-Tak
glue
scissors
cardboard

Cut four circles of cardboard about 5 cm larger in diameter than the ends of the cotton reels. Make a hole in the centre of each one and glue them on.

Push a cotton reel onto one of the sticks so that it rests in the middle. Then cut two lengths of string about half a metre long and tie them each side of the reel as shown. Fix the free ends of the string to the upper bannister rail. This is the top pulley.

To make the bottom pulley, cut a length of string four times the height of the top bannister rail and tie one end of it near the middle of the second stick. Push the second cotton reel onto the stick, fixing some Blu-Tak on the other side to stop it slipping off, but allowing it to move freely.

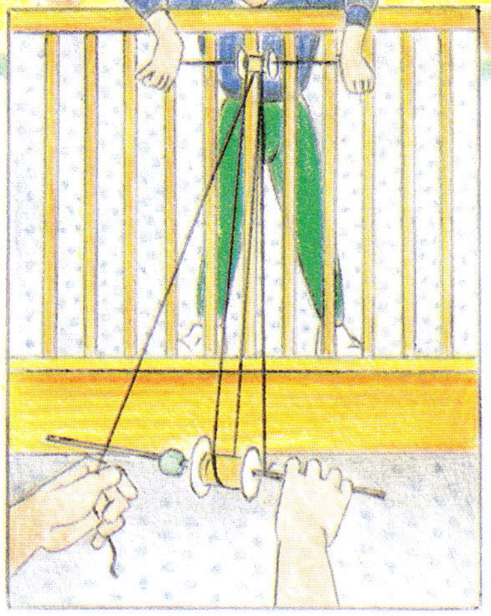

Get a friend to hold this stick just below the one already fixed to the bannisters, then wind the long string over the top reel, down and round the bottom reel, over the top reel again and finally let it go down to the ground. Go down and lower the pulley as your friend lets it go.

Attach the carrier bag to the stick, put your things in it and wind up the string. As you do, all your things will be taken easily upstairs.

Why it works

Pulleys are machines which allow you to use less effort to move a heavy load. Although you are using less effort than if you lifted your things, you will find that the length of string you pull will be three times the height that your things have travelled. The more pulleys you have on a system, the heavier the load you can lift.

Disco Dancers

You will need:
shoe box with a lid
scissors
masking tape
2 thin plastic straws
2 wider plastic straws
1 flexible straw
2 pins

Near one end of the box make two holes in each side, opposite each other, large enough for the wider straw to fit and to turn freely.

To make cogs, cut the lid in two sections about a quarter of the way along. From the larger part cut four circles about 4 cm across and make the edges wavy. Make a hole in the middle of two of them large enough for the wider straw to fit. Push the straw through the hole in one side of the box, through the two cogs and through the other side of the box.

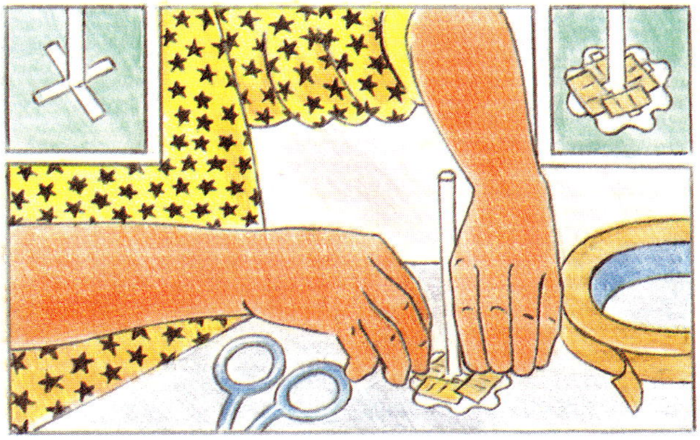

Take the two thin straws and make four slits in one end of each straw. Bend the sections back and tape them firmly to the middles of the other circles. Rest the lid on the box. Near each edge, directly above the straw pole, make a hole large enough for the straws to turn freely.

Take one of the wider straws, cut it in half, make four slits in one end of each half, bend the sections back and tape them over the holes in the lid. Push the cogs along the pole so that one is below each hole.

Lift the lid and push the two thin straws up through the wider straws. The cogs attached to them should rest on top of the lower ones, as shown. Push a pin through each thin straw just where it sticks out above the wider one, to keep it in position. Tape the lower cogs firmly to their pole so that they turn with it and finally tape down the lid.

Cut out two dancing figures and tape them to the thin straws. To make a handle, fix a small section of the flexible straw over the end of the pole. As you turn it the dancers will move around.

Why it works

When two objects move against each other, friction is always there trying to stop the movement. As you turn the handle, the cogs on the pole touch the dancers' cogs making them turn. This is because the friction between the two cogs prevents them slipping. This demonstrates how cogs are used in machinery to change the direction of movement.

Swirls and Whirls

You will need:
wooden baseboard
assorted jam jar lids
nails 1.5–2 cm long
hammer
drawing paper
felt-tip pens
masking tape
self-adhesive sticky pads
large cup hook
wide elastic bands or reel of fabric plaster

Make circles of paper by drawing round each lid. Cut them out and find and mark the centre of each circle (see diagram on page 5). Set them aside remembering which circle fits which lid.

Stick three layers of self-adhesive pads at roughly equal intervals around the edge of each lid. Then tape all round them.

Glue the circles to their lids and decorate them with patterns.

Place one of the larger lids near the edge of the baseboard and hammer a nail through the centre point. Slightly enlarge the hole by moving the lid about. Make another hole near the edge of the lid and push the cup hook into it to act as a handle. Turn it and the lid should whirl round.

Take the next lid and position it so that it is pushing against the first lid. Hammer it in place. Turn the handle and both lids should spin. If they are difficult to turn, slightly enlarge the hole in the second lid until you can get them turning freely together. Do the same with a third lid. See how many you can get moving at once.

If the lids begin to lose contact with each other, fix an elastic band or strip of fabric plaster round the edge to increase the friction.

Why it works

The sticky pads on the lids form teeth that interlock, so that when the first lid is turned, it drives the second lid around and so on. Each cog will turn the next one in the opposite direction, and smaller lids turn faster than larger ones.

Make a Paddle Boat

You will need:

smooth plastic soft drinks bottle with a lid
2 sticks
masking tape or waterproof tape
plastic ice-cream tub lid or
 similar (rectangular)
scissors
elastic band

Tape the sticks, one each side of the bottle about three-quarters of the way down, making sure they stick out behind.

Cut four rectangles from the ice-cream tub lid to make the paddle. The size will depend on the size of your bottle. For a 250 ml bottle you will need 5 x 3 cm paddles, for a 2 litre bottle approximately 8 x 5 cm paddles. Fold the rectangles in half lengthways and tape them together all round to form the paddle.

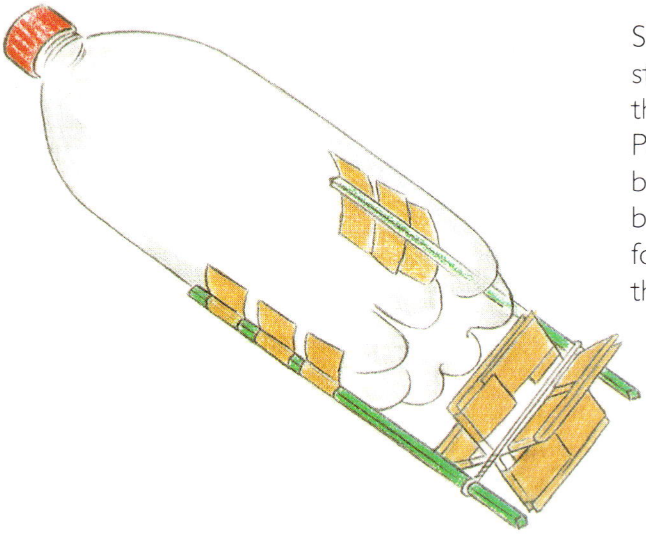

Slip the elastic band over the ends of the sticks. It should fit comfortably between the sticks without being too stretched. Position the wheel in between the elastic band and wind it up anti-clockwise. Let the boat go in the bath and it will shoot forwards. If you wind the paddle clockwise the boat will go backwards.

Why it works
The boat is driven by the energy stored in the twisted elastic band. In this case, as the elastic unwinds the paddle turns, pushing the water backwards and the boat forwards.

Creepy Crawlies

You will need:

cotton reel
stub end of a candle about 1 cm thick
2 matchsticks or cocktail sticks broken into approximately 1 and 2 centimetre lengths
masking tape
sheet of paper
small saucer
scissors
crayons or paints
small safety pin
elastic band about 4 cm long
glue
corkscrew

Neaten the candle stub with the scissors and using a corkscrew or the scissors if they are pointed, carefully enlarge the hole down the middle. Pull out the wick and make a small groove across one end of the stub. This will hold the longer matchstick in position.

Loop one end of the elastic band over the shorter matchstick and hold it in place while you loop the other end through the safety pin. Thread the pin down through the cotton reel and the candle stub. Fix the end of the elastic with the longer matchstick, resting it in the groove in the candle. Remove the safety pin.

Tape over the short stick to keep it in position and tape round the edges of the cotton reel to give it a better grip as it moves around.

Draw round the saucer and make a paper cone as you made the funnels on page 5.

Cut out large paper insect shapes, colour them and glue them to the top of the cone, bending the legs down to disguise the cone.

Wind up the cotton reel by turning the matchstick round and round until you can feel that the elastic is fairly tight. Put the reel down, quickly place your insect on top and watch it crawl around!

Why it works
The insect is driven along by the energy stored in the twisted elastic band. The energy is slowly released as the elastic band unwinds.

Build Yourself a Paper House

You will need:
a pile of newspapers of varying sizes
masking tape

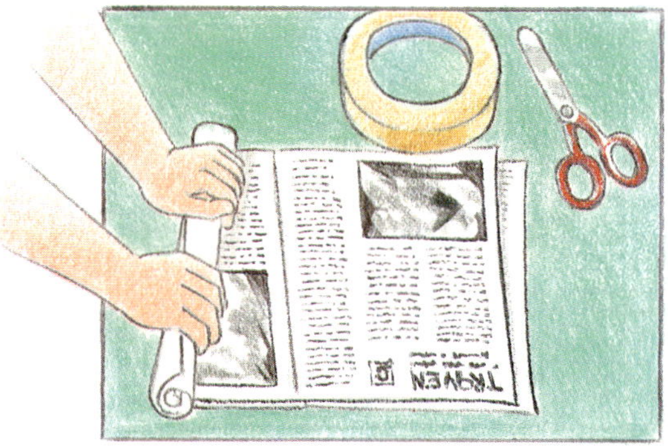

Tightly roll up a sheet of newspaper taping the end down firmly. If you have trouble making the roll rigid enough, use three sheets together or roll them round a plant support stick and remove it afterwards.

By using a variety of large and small newspapers or rolling them diagonally as well as straight, you can make different-sized rolls.

When you have a large pile of rolls, tape them into triangles, squares and rectangles. From these shapes you will be able to build a variety of structures – from domes to wigwams. The smaller the shapes are, the stronger the finished structure will be.

When you have finished your house, tape sheets of newspaper over the structure to make it private.

Why it works

These paper buildings do not collapse because the paper has been made stronger by rolling it.

A Suspension Bridge

You will need:
packet of straws
ball of thin string
masking tape
drawing pins
sheet of cardboard the length of the bridge
scissors
2 large rectangles of strong cardboard or wood to act as tower bases

Cut two straws in half and tape them into a square. Take four straws and tape one at each corner of the square, then tape the tops together to form a pyramid. This is the first tower.

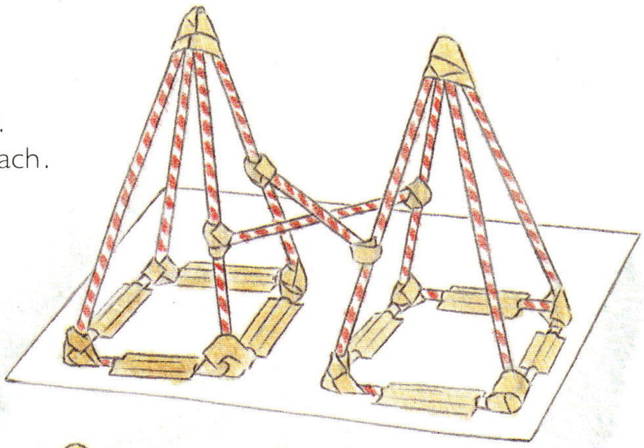

Tape it near one end of a baseboard and make three more towers in the same way. Attach these to the baseboards, two on each.

Tape two straws about half way down between each pair of towers to make a platform for the roadway.

When you have decided how long the bridge is to be, cut two pieces of string that will stretch from one base, over the top of a tower, across to the other tower and down to the base on the opposite side. Fix these in place, tying them to the top of the towers and pinning them to the bases.

Cut the cardboard roadway and make holes down either side about 2 cm apart. Rest it between the platforms and weigh it down to keep it in place while you finish making the bridge. Weigh down the bases as well, if necessary.

Cut a piece of string twice as long as the bridge, tie one end to the string at the top of a tower then thread it down through the first hole in the roadway, up through the next hole, over the string rail, down through the next hole and so on. Finish by tying the other end to the string at the top of the tower on the other side. Do the same for the other side of the roadway.

Why it works
In this suspension bridge the towers do not collapse because they are built to be strong enough to withstand the tension or stretching forces in the string. Because the roadway is held up by the strings you do not need pillars in the middle of the bridge and larger widths can be spanned.

Remove the weights, make cardboard ramps up to the roadway, and your bridge is ready for use.

Ghostly Lights

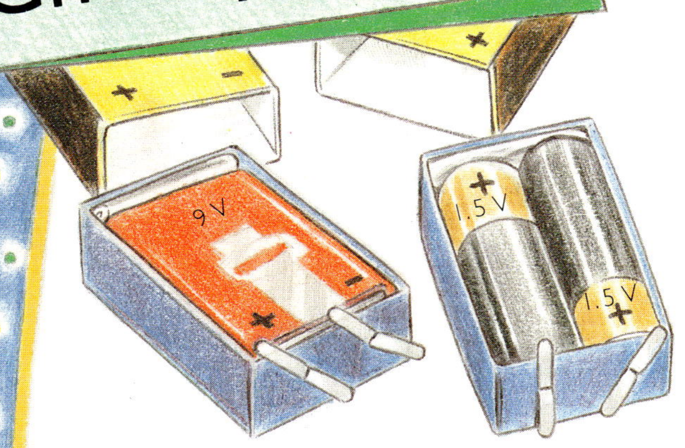

First make the battery holder.
Place the battery in the matchbox and mark where the two connecting points (terminals) touch the end. Take the battery out and at each of these points push one butterfly clip through the box.

Replace the battery so that the terminals touch the clips. You may need to wedge some paper at the other end to make sure the battery always touches the clips. Slide the lid on the box.

You will need:
sheet of cardboard
paints
4 LEDs (Light Emitting Diodes – these can be bought cheaply in electrical spares shops and come in red, yellow and green)
plastic-coated wire for batteries
wire cutters
scissors
masking tape
9 volt battery holder
(made from a
matchbox,
2 butterfly clips,
self-adhesive labels)

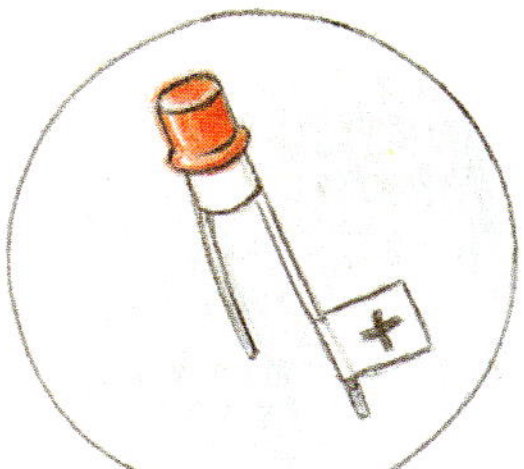

Each LED has a long wire and a short wire already attached to it. Make sure you write a + sign on the labels and stick them to the long wires as soon as you take the LEDs out of the packet.

Now the picture:
Paint a picture on the cardboard, and when you have decided where you want the lights, make small holes and push the LEDs through so that the wires are behind.

Cut three lengths of battery wire so that you can connect all the lights up together.

Use the wire cutters to strip off 1 cm of the plastic coating at each end of the wires.

Connect these lengths of wires to the LEDs by twisting them together. It is important to connect the long wire of one LED to the short wire of the next one. Tape each join to the cardboard.

Now measure and cut two pieces of wire to reach from the two end lights to the battery holder. Strip 1 cm of plastic coating from each end of the wires and connect them up. The + terminal on the battery should connect up with a + wire of an LED and the – terminal with a short wire.

You can make the lights flash by leaving one of the wires to the battery loose and just pressing it against the butterfly clip when you want it to flash.

Attach your picture to a T-shirt and you can wear your lights!

Never connect just one or two LEDs to a 9 volt battery or you will damage them.

A 9 volt battery is not powerful enough to cause an electric shock, nor can it generate enough heat to cause a spark or fire. Of course you must never experiment with mains electricity.

Why it works
The power stored in a battery can only be released and harnessed when a complete circuit is made. This is done by connecting the lights to the + and – terminals on the battery with wires.

You can alter the battery holder to house two 1.5 volt penlight batteries (enough to light up just one LED). For instructions, see page 26.

Who's There?

You will need:
2 x 1.5 volt penlight batteries in a holder
3 volt buzzer or bell (available from electrical spares shops)
plastic-coated wire for batteries
thick corrugated cardboard
aluminium foil
scissors
wire cutters
masking tape

Adapt the holder on page 24 by fixing a strip of aluminium foil across the opposite end to the clips. Place the batteries side by side, with the positive ends in opposite directions. Make sure they are always touching the clips and the foil.

Cut two squares of cardboard about 8 cm x 8 cm and make a hole through the centre of each square. Then cut two pieces of wire long enough to reach from underneath a mat outside your door to the place where you are going to keep the buzzer inside your room.

Using the wire cutters, strip off 1 cm of the plastic coating at each end of the wires.

Push the end of one wire through one of the holes in the cardboard and bend it flat against the other side. Position a 2 cm square of aluminium foil over it and tape all round it. Do the same with the other square of cardboard and the other length of wire.

Cut four ridges out of corrugated cardboard and stick the wired squares together, using the ridges to stop the foil pieces touching unless they are pressed together. This part of the alarm goes underneath the mat outside the room.

Using a length of wire that has 1 cm of the plastic coating at each end stripped off, join the battery holder and the buzzer together.

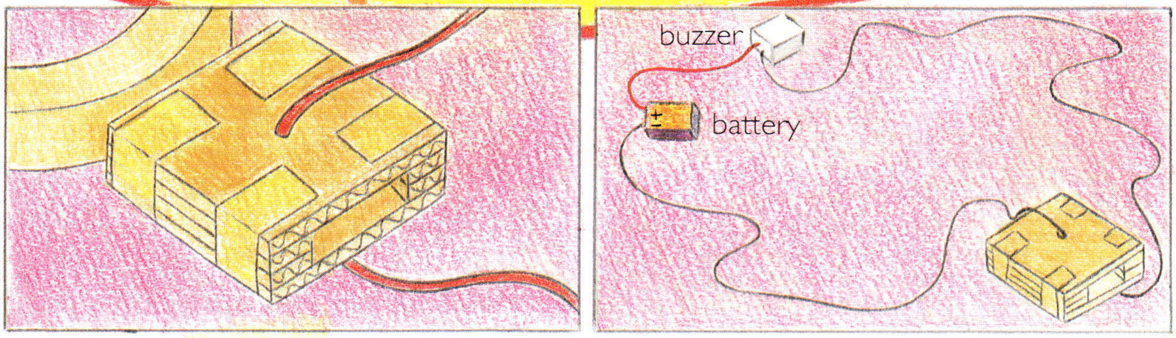

Now connect the wires from the section outside the door: one wire to the battery and one wire to the buzzer. Tape the joins. The red wire from the buzzer goes to the positive terminal and the black wire goes to the negative terminal.

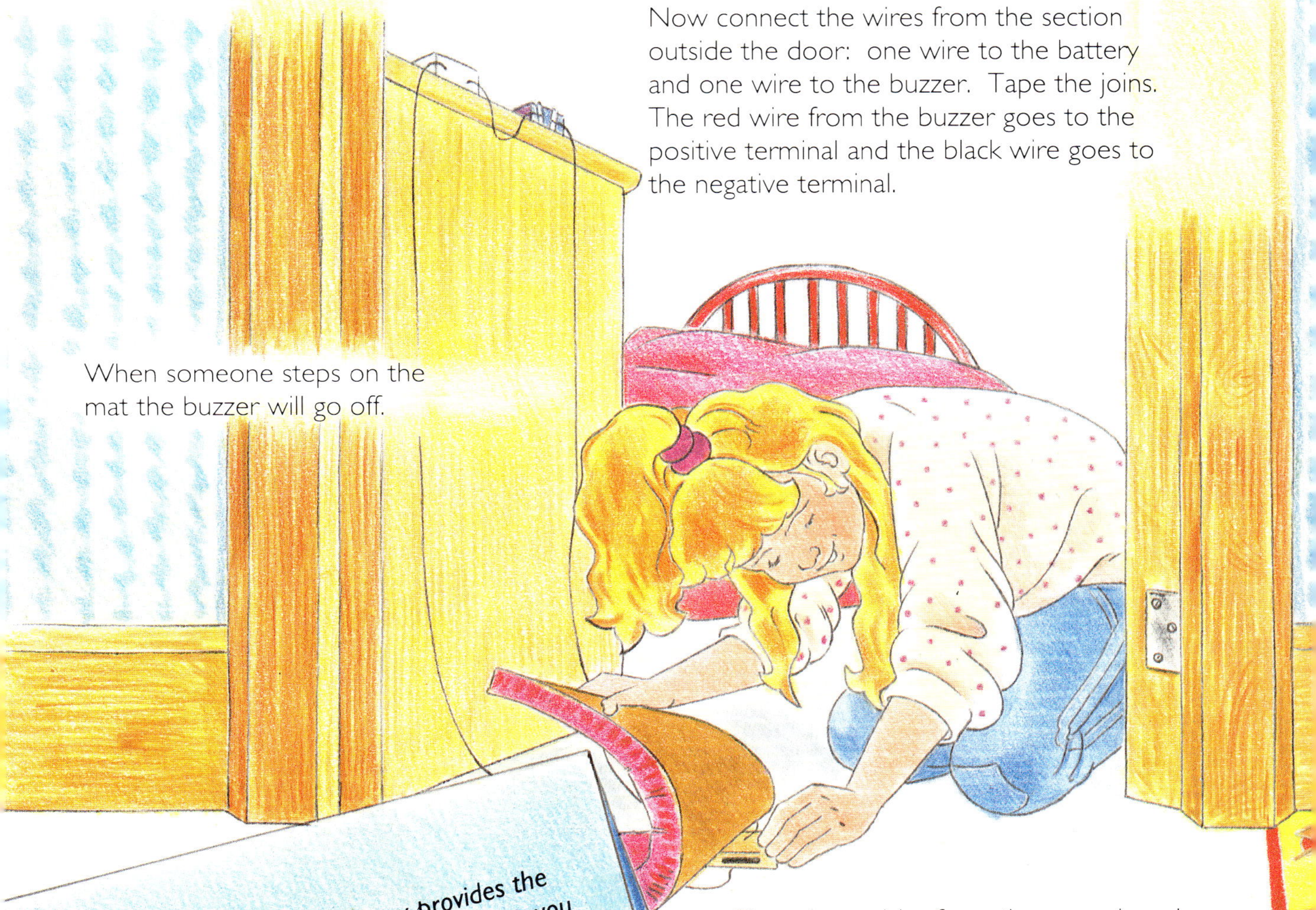

When someone steps on the mat the buzzer will go off.

Why it works
As in Ghostly Lights the battery provides the energy to make the buzzer work. When you step on the mat the two pieces of foil touch, making the electric circuit complete, and the buzzer makes a noise. When you step off, the pieces of foil spring apart breaking the circuit and stopping the buzzer.

There is no risk of creating a spark and therefore a fire from these wires under the mat. The voltage is too low. Wires from a normal domestic electrical supply must never be put under carpets.

Make a Compass to Guide You

You will need:

small margarine tub or similar with a watertight lid
waterproof marker pen
large needle (e.g. darning/wool needle)
spare tub lid
magnet
cotton reel
plastic straw
masking tape or waterproof tape
scissors
waterproof glue
egg cup

Glue the cotton reel to the bottom of the tub. While it is setting, draw a circle round the egg cup on the spare tub lid and cut it out. Make four slits in one end of the straw, bend the sections back, then tape these to the underside of the plastic circle.

Cut the other end of the straw so that the circle will stand about 2 cm above the cotton reel when it is slotted in the hole.

To magnetize the needle, stroke it 20 times with the magnet, using a circular motion, always starting at the same end and always being careful to lift the magnet off the needle after each stroke. Afterwards make sure you put the magnet well away from the needle.

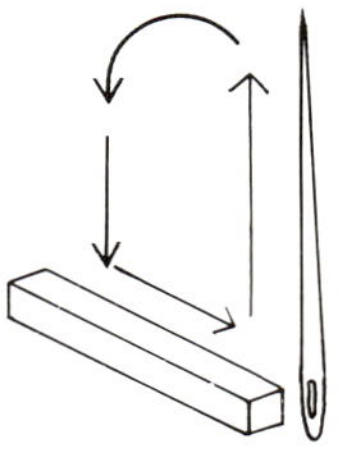

Tape the needle to the plastic circle and slot the straw into the cotton reel. Fill the tub with water so that the plastic circle just floats and moves around freely.

The needle will point north/south. Use the position of the sun in the sky to help you work out which is which.

If you have a watertight lid you will be able to use your compass to guide you on walks.

Why it works
When you stroke the needle with a magnet it becomes magnetic also. All magnets point to the north pole when allowed to swing freely because the strong magnetic force of the earth always pulls them in this direction. As long as the needle is not dropped or knocked it will remain magnetized.

Will the Mountaineer Fall Off?

You will need:
short pencil about 5 cm long
2 straws about 10 cm long
scissors
Blu-Tak
drawing paper
felt-tip pens
masking tape
pen or pencil which has a wide flat top

Firmly tape the two straws to the pencil so that they hang down at an angle and are rigid.

Wrap a smallish piece of Blu-Tak around the bottom of the pencil just above the point and stick two fairly large equal lumps onto the end of each straw.

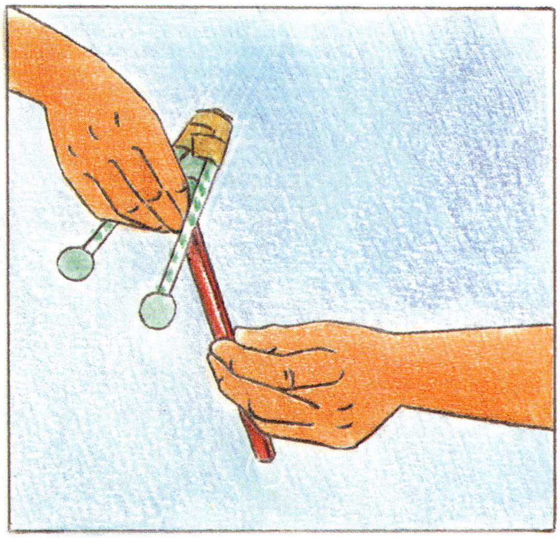

Test whether the whole thing balances upright on a flat-topped pen. If it does not, adjust the balance by adding or taking away Blu-Tak from the ends of the straws.

Fold the drawing paper in half and draw a mountaineer to fit over the pencil and straws. Colour it in on both sides, and cut it out leaving it joined at the head.

Fold the mountaineer over the pencil, pressing him into the Blu-Tak at the base to keep him in position.

Balance him on the pen top and see how far you can tip it before he falls off. If you stick the pen into a lump of Blu-Tak on the table you can also spin him round. You can experiment with pencils and straws of different sizes.

Why it works

The earth exerts a force on everything, pulling objects towards itself. This force is called gravity. The centre of gravity of an object is the point at which this gravitational force appears to act. The mountaineer will not fall because the two weights he is carrying make most of his weight below the pencil top on which he is balancing. It is important to take into consideration the centre of gravity of any object you design, to make sure that it is stable.

Make the Octopus Go in the Cave

Bend the straw round as far as it will go and cut the ends off so that you are left with a length of about 5 cm.

You will need:
2 litre plastic soft drinks bottle with a lid
flexible straw
paper clips
margarine tub lid
Plasticine/Blu-Tak
waterproof pen
scissors
black paper
large bowl of water

Cut the octopus out from the margarine tub lid. Its body should be about 2.5 cm long and its legs 2.5 cm long too. Attach it to the straw using the paperclips. One half of each clip should go up inside the straw. Draw in the eyes with the pen and then test that the octopus floats upright by putting it in the bowl of water. If it does not, add another clip or fix a small piece of Blu-Tak near the base of the body until it does.

Cut a rocky shape from the black paper and tape it round the bottom of the bottle. Fill the bottle with water and put in the octopus. Make sure the bottle is full to overflowing then screw the lid on tightly.

Why it works
When you squeeze the bottle, water is forced into the straw making the octopus heavier so that it sinks. When you release the pressure on the bottle the water comes out of the straw making the octopus lighter again so that it floats to the top.

Squeeze the bottle hard and the octopus will dive down into the cave, let go and it will float up to the top of the bottle.